CANADIAN TEXTILES

*The object of this series is to present a Survey of World Textiles, each
volume dealing with a separate country.*

Other volumes are to follow and will be announced from time to time.

CANADIAN TEXTILES

by

J. H. THOMPSON

F. LEWIS, PUBLISHERS, LIMITED

LEIGH-ON-SEA

Printed at the Dolphin Press, Brighton

Introduction

CANADIAN TEXTILES are as modern as today, the products of an industry that has its roots deep in the history of the country. From the homespuns of its early settlers, to the newest chemical fibres, her textiles have matched the exciting development of this young nation.

As early as 1667, the first Intendant of 'New France', one Jean Talon, wrote home to France that '*At present everything necessary to dress me from head to foot is being made in Canada*'. At that time, production was limited to spinning and weaving in the homes of the settlers, but in the nineteenth century, the industry began to take the form into which it has developed today.

Unlike many countries, Canada is fortunate in having her own abundant supply of the raw materials necessary to the production of man-made fibres and modern chemical finishes, and is as close as any major country to the sources of natural fibres. She is thus able to offer vastly improved fabrics of both manufactured yarns and traditional fibres, plus a whole new family of man-made yarns.

Dramatic contrasts can also be found in the textiles of the country. The collective arts, crafts and tastes of the peoples of many lands who form the population of Canada are reflected in the colours and exciting new concepts in design; in the infinite variety of cotton and wool yarns and fabrics, and in the diversity of finishes and surface effects which make them distinctive. The vivid colourings of Canada's lakes and forests are reflected in prints on cottons and other fabrics giving them a 'fresh' appeal in other lands. North American Indian and Eskimo designs vie with those of Scandinavian or Asian origin in popular appeal. Fine woollens inspired by Quebec 'Habitant' designs are produced alongside the more traditional patterns of European derivation.

One of the first woollen mills in Canada was established in 1820 near Georgetown, Ontario; this was followed in 1827 by a more up-to-date mill at L'Arcadie, Quebec. 1845 saw the opening of the first cotton mill at Sherbrooke, and from this time onward the industry grew up along the St. Lawrence and St. Maurice rivers in the Province of Quebec, while in Ontario a like growth was establishing itself along the Ottawa and Grand River Valleys.

Today there are seven hundred mills in Canada, with some seventy-five thousand employees, engaged in producing textiles to the value of about $800 millions annually. These mills are not only producing both natural and man-made fibres in a great variety of yarns, but they are also spinning, weaving, knitting, printing and finishing fabrics for all purposes, all outstanding in quality and technical accomplishment.

Immigration, apart from increasing the settled population of Canada, has also played a very important part in the textile manufactures of Canada—apart from the creation of a larger demand for these goods, it brought to Canada many skilled textile workers from Great Britain and other European centres. Today the industry trains its own technicians in two textile schools.

The beginning of the twentieth century marked the establishment in Canada of factory production clothing of all kinds to meet the growing needs of the increasing population. The fashion shows of Canadian made and styled clothes for both men and women are a highlight wherever they are given, comparable with those of any country.

Canadian textiles recently won plaudits in Britain, long a stronghold of quality fabrics. Canada's easy-care cottons, and fabrics of man-made fibres were found 'equal, if not superior' in colour, prints and designs to British fabrics of the same types. Furnishing fabrics also created excitement during their first modest invasion of British markets by Canadian manufacturers.

The development of Canadian textiles has kept abreast of the country's changing way of life. For instance, the huge post-war swing to suburban living, increased prosperity and more leisure time having resulted in a fantastic growth of casual and sports clothes. These materials have talents as varied as resistance to blazing sun to protection against Arctic cold. Thus Canada today offers a bewildering array of fabrics for every purpose, new beauty and practicability having made former luxuries commonplace; for instance, laces once almost exclusive to the wealthy are today a fashion fabric brought within the price range of everyone.

It is hoped that this volume will serve to give some indication to the reader, of the design, quality and diversity of products currently being marketed in Canada.

Finally I would like to express thanks to Mr. W. M. Berry, President of the Primary Textile Institute, Montreal, to Madelaine Marcoux, Directress of Centrale d'Artisanat du Quebec, Montreal, for their help and interest, and also to the various Companies who so kindly contributed materials, and whose book this really is. The photographs are by Armour Landry of Montreal and Leslie G. Arnold of Leigh-on-Sea, England.

Descriptive Notes
on the Illustrations

Figure 1   QUEBEC SCENE. Hooked rug 28 by 36 inches. Designed and worked by Jeanne d'Arc Fortin, Pointe au Pic, P.Q.

Figure 2   HOOKED RUG, 54 by 76 inches. Scene in Quebec depicting the gathering of the sap from maple trees in early spring. Designed and worked by George Edward Trembley, of Pointe au Pic, P.Q. From the permanent collection of Centrale d'Artistanat du Quebec, Montreal.

Figure 3   HOOKED RUG, 28 by 35 inches. Designed and worked by the Grenfell Labrador Industries.

Figure 4   HOOKED RUG, 48 by 52 inches. Designed and worked by Mrs. Ulderic Collard, Wattonville, P.Q. From the permanent collection of Centrale d'Artisanat du Quebec, Montreal.

Figure 5   This shows part of the boardroom of Centrale d'Artisanat du Quebec, Montreal. The rug, 14 by 24 feet, is all wool braided, and designed by Terese Chabot, St. Antoine sur Richelieu, Quebec. The all-wool drapery and upholstery fabrics hand-woven by Au Terroir Engr., St. Hyacinthe, P.Q.

Figure 6   Group of hand-woven 'CATALOGNE' rugs. Originally woven from rags. Today most of the weavers use cotton strips. (*Top left*) Designed and woven by Terese Chabot. (*Top right*) Designed and woven by Mrs. Paule Dorais, Acton Vale, P.Q. (*Bottom left*) Designed and woven by Mrs. Lucien Levesque, of St. Clements County. (*Bottom right*) Designed and woven by Terese Chabot, St. Antoine sur Richelieu.

Figure 7   'PLAZA' acetate warp viscose fill. Screen printed by Montreal Fast Print Ltd. Designed by Canadian Textile Studio. From Sears-Golick (Canada) Fabrics.

Figure 8   'ESSEX', a 45-inch screen-printed drapery by Montreal Fast Print Ltd., on a 40 per cent acetate, 60 per cent viscose fabric. The design by Canadian Textile Studio, Montreal. From Daly and Morin Ltd., Lachine, P.Q.

Figure 9   'TROY', a novelty weave of acetate and spun viscose. 45-inch machine screen print by Montreal Fast Print Ltd. From Sheftex Corporation, Montreal, P.Q.

Figure 10   'LINFIELD', roller-printed drapery, printed by Riverdale Town House; fibreglass. The design by Yvonne Ligus. From Riverdale Town House Fabrics, Montreal.

Figure 11   'DRESDEN', a screen-printed drapery by Montreal Fast Print Ltd. 100 per cent Arnel warp. 50 per cent arnel, 50 per cent viscose fill. Designed by E. Heidersdorf. From Daly & Morin Ltd., Lachine, P.Q.

Figure 12   'VALMOUNT', a 45-inch furnishing fabric of 43.5 per cent acetate, 56.5 per cent viscose; screen printed. Designed by E. Heidersdorf, Point Claire, P.Q. From Daly & Morin Ltd., Lachine, P.Q.

Figure 13   'ARABELLA', roller-printed on an acetate and viscose fabric by Riverdale Town House. Designed by Yvonne Ligus. From Riverdale Town House Fabrics, Montreal.

Figures 14 and 15   (*Top*) 'GLAMOUR' and (*Bottom*) 'PATRICIA'. Two screen-printed furnishing draperies, on a 43.5 per cent acetate, 56.5 per cent viscose; 45 inch. Designed by E. Heidersdorf, Point Claire, P.Q. From Daly & Morin Ltd., Lachine, P.Q.

Figure 16   'SUNDRIDGE', heavy viscose pebble cloth. Designed by Thor Hansen, Ontario. Screen printed by Montreal Fast Print Ltd., Montreal. Courtesy of A. B. Caya Ltd., Kitchener, Ontario.

Figure 17   This decorative scenic drapery on a mohair, viscose and acetate fabric, is printed and woven by Bruck Mills Ltd. From Val-Abel Textiles Ltd., Montreal.

Figure 18   'BIRCHBANK', designed by E. Heidersdorf; a screen print by Montreal Fast Print Ltd., on a fabric of 100 per cent arnel warp, 50 per cent arnel and 50 per cent viscose fill; 43 inches wide. From Daly & Morin Ltd., Lachine, P.Q.

Figure 19   'SONIC', 100 per cent arnel fabric. Screen printed by Montreal Fast Print Ltd. Designed by Canadian Textile Studio. From Sears-Golick (Canada) Fabrics, Montreal.

Figure 20   'AIDA', natural flowers combined with a contemporary setting make this 45-inch drapery. Designed by Canadian Textile Studio, Montreal, and screen-printed by Montreal Fast Print Ltd. From Daly & Morin Ltd., Lachine, P.Q.

Figure 21   'GARLAND', a screen-printed drapery on a 43.5 per cent acetate and 56.5 per cent viscose material. The design by E. Heidersdorf, Point Claire, P.Q. From Daly & Morin Ltd., Lachine, P.Q.

Figure 22   'MANOR', a machine screen-printed furnishing by Montreal Fast Print Ltd., 100 per cent arnel warp, viscose fill fabric. 46/47 inch width. From Sheftex Corporation, Montreal, P.Q.

Figure 23   'TREND'; designed by Canadian Textile Studio of Montreal, this novelty weave of acetate and spun viscose yarn is machine-printed by Montreal Fast Print Ltd., 45 inches. From Sheftex Corporation, Montreal, P.Q.

Figure 24   This contemporary design is by Canadian Textile Studio, of Montreal. Printed on type 'F' acetate warp and spun viscose material by Duplan of Canada Ltd. From Sears-Golick (Canada) Fabrics, Montreal, P.Q.

Figure 25   'PARKVIEW', 45-inch screen-printed drapery, on a 43.5 per cent acetate, 56.5 per cent viscose spun fabric. The design by E. Heidersdorf, Point Claire, P.Q. From Daly & Morin Ltd., Lachine, P.Q.

Figure 26   'ATWOOD', a 36-inch all-cotton 'bark' cloth. This drapery is roller printed in vat colours. The design by Canadian Textile Studio, Montreal. From Daly & Morin Ltd., Lachine, P.Q.

Figures 27 and 28   (*Top*) 'ARCADE', (*Bottom*) 'MOBILE'. Two screen prints, by Montreal Fast Print Ltd., on an arnel and viscose fibre cloth. Both are good examples of Canadian design, one based on an architectural garden shelter, the other a stage backcloth. From A. B. Caya Ltd., Kitchener, Ontario.

Figure 29   'NAVARRA', roller printed on a fibreglass fabric by Riverdale Town House. Designed by Yvonne Ligus. From Riverdale Town House Fabrics, Montreal.

Figure 30   French Provincial scroll design by Canadian Textile Studio, Montreal. Screen printed on antique satin weave of acetate warp with viscose fill. Printed by Montreal Fast Print Ltd. From Sears-Golick (Canada) Fabrics, Montreal.

Figures 31 and 32   (*Top*) 'NAUTICAL' and (*Bottom*) 'SMALL FRY'. Two roller-printed all-cotton 'bark' cloth draperies. Designed by Canadian Textile Studio, Montreal printed all-cotton 'bark' cloth draperies. Designed by Canadian Textile Studio, Montreal. From Daly & Morin Ltd., Lachine, P.Q.

Figure 33   Screen printed boucle. Designed by Canadian Textile Studio, Montreal, and printed by Montreal Fast Print Ltd. From Daly & Morin Ltd., Lachine, P.Q.

Figure 34   Multicoloured printed net curtaining on 100 per cent terylene fibre from C.I.L. The fabric woven by Bruck Mills Ltd., Montreal. The design by Canadian Textile Studio, Montreal. From St. Louis Textiles Ltd., Montreal.

Figure 35   Screen print on linen. The design by the Montreal Fast Print Studio. From A. B. Caya Ltd., Kitchener, Ontario.

Figure 36   Multicoloured printed net curtaining on 100 per cent terylene fibre from C.I.L. The fabric woven by Bruck Mills Ltd., Montreal, the design by Canadian Textile Studio, Montreal. From St. Louis Textiles Ltd., Montreal.

Figures 37 and 38   Two 36-inch roller machine prints on cotton with Everglaze finish. Printed by Dominion Textiles Ltd., both designed by Canadian Textile Studio of Montreal. From Daly & Morin Ltd., Lachine, P.Q.

Figures 39 and 40   'DRESDEN', standard 80 square, 39-inch Percale cotton 4-yard cloth. Both of these cotton prints designed by Fields & Currie Ltd., Montreal. From the Wabasso Co. Ltd., Montreal.

Figures 41 and 42   Screen printed on an all-cotton sailcloth by Montreal Fast Print Ltd., Montreal. From A. B. Caya Ltd., Kitchener, Ontario.

Figures 43 and 44   Two all-cotton multicoloured prints, both produced in a sportswear range of patterns. The designs by Fields & Currie Ltd., of Montreal. From Dominion Textile Co. Ltd., Montreal.

Figure 45   An all-cotton shirting for sports wear. A very colourful print. Designed by Fields & Currie Ltd., From Dominion Textile Co. Ltd., Montreal.

Figures 46, 47 and 48   (*Left and Right*) 'SURRAH' Two roller-printed dress materials by Coramil. (*Centre*) 'MAGIC CREPE'. Roller printed for ladies dresses and blouses. All three on a 100 per cent acetate fabric. From Consolidated Textiles Ltd., Montreal.

Figure 49   This 36-inch cotton with Everglaze finish in washable colours is roller printed by Dominion Textiles Ltd., the design by Canadian Textile Studio, Montreal. From Daly & Morin Ltd., Lachine, P.Q.

Figures 50 and 51   (*Left*) This is a roller-printed dress fabric in 100 per cent terylene 'Batiste'* fibre by C.I.L. (*Right*) 100 per cent terylene crepe woven with fibre from C.I.L. for blouses and dresses. Both from Consolidated Textiles Ltd., Montreal.

---

* Originated from Jean Baptiste, a French weaver.

Figures 52 and 53 (*Left*) 'SURRAH' roller printed in three colours on a 100 per cent acetate fabric by Coramil. The design in pink and red with black outline on a white ground. (*Right*) 'MAGIC CREPE', 100 per cent acetate roller print for blouses and dresses; multicoloured. Both from Consolidated Textiles Ltd., Montreal.

Figures 54, 55 and 56 (*Top left*) 100 per cent cotton, 'LUSTRETONE' range. Black and white design for ladies dresses, sports shirts, etc. (*Bottom left*) 100 per cent acetate fabric by Coramil. One of the range of 'SURRAH' roller prints. (*Right*) Designed for men's sports wear and woven from rayon viscose and cotton. All from Consolidated Textiles Ltd., Montreal.

Figures 57 and 58 (*Left*) All-cotton print for sports shirts. Designed by Fields & Currie Ltd., Montreal. From Dominion Textile Co. Ltd., Montreal. (*Right*) This design of Sagittarius the Centaur motif is roller printed on cotton and intended for ladies blouses and men's sports shirts. From Consolidated Textiles Ltd., Montreal.

Figure 59 'MARDI GRAS', an all-cotton print. Designed by Fields & Currie Ltd. of Montreal for skirts and dresses. Our illustration shows how extremely well the black and white design lends itself to making-up. From Dominion Textile Co. Ltd., Montreal.

Figure 60 'MAORI', flannelette. Standard flannelette construction for the Canadian market; 40½ grey, 3.75 yard cloth, wove 42/44. The design by Fields & Currie Ltd., Montreal. From the Wabasso Cotton Co. Ltd., Montreal.

Figure 61 Suitable for both lingerie and children's wear, these seven examples were designed by Canadian Textile Studio, Montreal. The fabric composed of 70 per cent 40 dernier terylene and 30 per cent nylon. The Terylene Polyester fibre by Canadian Industries Ltd. The white pattern being the nylon. Piece dyed after weaving; Terylene resists the dye, thus leaving the pattern white. From Springdale Mills Ltd., Montreal.

Figure 62 100 per cent dyed viscose yarn. For men's sports shirts etc. From Bruck Mills Ltd., Montreal.

Figures 63 and 64 Woven fabrics composed of rayon viscose and cotton. For sports shirts and other sports wear. From Consolidated Textiles Ltd., Montreal.

Figures 65 and 66 Two woven damasks in fancy weaves, acetate warp, solution dyed rayon fill. (*Left*) is called 'COLUMBIA' and is in shades of lilac. (*Right*) known as 'FINESSE' in shades of nutmeg browns. From Sheftex Corporation, Montreal, P.Q.

Figures 67 and 68 Two all-cotton cloths, 60 inches wide, 10/12 ozs. For sportswear, also extensively used as rainwear after treatment to repel water. From Artex Woollens Ltd., Hespeler, Ontario.

Figures 69, 70, 71 and 72   Four hand-woven fancy weaves. (*Top right*) Linen cotton warp, linen wool fill. (*Right*) Wool, linen, cotton and rayon warp; rayon, viscose and spun wool fill. Straight Tabby weave. (*Bottom right*) Oatmeal wool, woollen spun warp, rayon viscose, boucle fill; straight Tabby weave. (*Left centre*) Rayon boucle linen, viscose rayon and cotton boucle warp; wool and linen fill. All designed by Margareta Steeves. From Karen Bulow Ltd., Montreal, P.Q.

Figures 73 and 74 (*Top right*) All-wool brushed loop type, for sports wear, skirts, etc., 57 inches wide, 12½ ozs. Available in a variety of colours, brown, green, etc. (*Top left*) All worsted wool, 57 inches, bulky type made in assorted patterns. Suitable for sports wear, dresses, skirts. From Artex Woollens Ltd., Hespeler, Ontario.

Figures 75 and 76 (*Top*) 50 per cent wool rayon, 57 inches wide, 12½ ozs. Brushed cable stitch with overcheck, for Ladies skirts.
(*Bottom*) Hounds tooth pattern all worsted wool, 57 inches, bulky type, for sports wear, dresses, skirts. From Artex Woollens Ltd., Hespeler, Ontario.

Figures 77 and 78 (*Top right*) Wool and mohair long hair brushed fabric. (*Top left*) All wool brushed fabric. From Textile Weavers Ltd., Grand'mere, P.Q.

Figures 79 and 80   (*Top*) 100 per cent pure wool fabric, for men's 'Jack' shirts and sports wear. From J. A. Humphrey and Son Ltd., Moncton, N.B. (*Bottom*) 57 inch all worsted wool, for sports wear, dresses, skirts. From Artex Woollens Ltd., Hespeler, Ontario.

Figures 81, 82, 83, 84, 85 and 86   (*Top left*) 22-24 oz. coating, 80 per cent wool and 20 per cent viscose. From J. A. Humphrey and Son Ltd., Moncton, N.B. (*Bottom left*) Jacquard woven check of wool and rayon. From Textile Weavers, Grand'mere, Quebec. (*Top centre and bottom right*) All wool jacquard weaves. From Textile Weavers, Grand-'mere, Quebec. (*Top right*) Wool and rayon brushed cloth. From Textile Weavers, Grand'mere, Quebec. (*Bottom centre*) 19-20 oz. winter coating of 90 per cent wool and 10 per cent mohair. 'Collie' fabric available in a full colour range. From J. A. Humphrey and Son Ltd., Moncton, N.B.

Figures 87 and 88   (*Left*) All wool worsted, normal twist, 9 oz., 57 inch, for dress slacks, etc. (*Right*) All wool fancy stripe, bulky type dress fabric, 7 oz., 57 inch. From Artex Woollens Ltd., Hespeler, Ontario.

Figures 89 and 90   (*Top*) For sports wear comes this 11 oz., 50 per cent wool and rayon woven fabric. (*Bottom*) Fancy twill-weave for ladies skirts, 10¾ oz., 57 inch, all spun wool. From Artex Woollens Ltd., Hespeler, Ontario.

Figure 91   57 inch all worsted wool weave, bulky type, for sports wear, dresses and skirts in a variety of patterns. From Artex Woollens Ltd., Hespeler, Ontario.

Figure 92 'SARAN', the genetic name for Vynylidene Chloride fibre. It was first introduced in 1939 by the Dow Chemical Company, but is now produced by a great many yarn manufacturers. A limited amount of staple is produced but the bulk of production is in monofilament form in which it is available in a substantial range of pigmented colours. It is a stiff plastic type yarn having good chemical resistance, is non-inflammable and melts around 340 degrees Fahrenheit. It is quite resistant to sunlight and outdoor exposure and hence it is used in screening, outdoor furniture, etc. It is generally produced with a co-polymer of vinyl chloride. It is more expensive than either polyethyle or polypropylene. Yarn by Dow Chemical Co. Woven by Burlington Industries (Canada) Ltd.

Figures 93, 94 and 95 (*Top*) Chenille bedspread 95 by 103 inches. Multicoloured floral with hobnail design. (*below*) Chenille mat and bath set, the Mat 24 by 36 inches. Designed by May Edelstein. From Ideal Spread Company, Montreal.

Figure 96 'CHASUBLE', the motif of wheat and ostensorium. Designed, embroidered and made by Robert Gens and Co., Ltd. of Montreal. The fabric, an acetate warp with viscose fill by Hafner Fabrics Canada Ltd., Granby, P.Q.

Figure 97 'CHASUBLE', the Fish and Anchor designed by Robert Gens. The fabric an acetate warp with viscose fill woven by Hafner Fabrics Canada Ltd., Granby, P.Q. The garment embroidered and made by Robert Gens and Co. Ltd., Montreal.

Figure 98 The swing to tights is expected to gain even greater momentum with a wider variety of novelty patterns and colours in nylon stretch. These peppermint stripes are by Harvey Woods who introduced tights to Canada several years ago. The one size in a range of shades stretches to fit sizes 14 to 20. The retail price is about Five Canadian Dollars or approximately thirty-five shillings sterling. The yarn by Dupont of Canada.

Figure 99 Sitting on top of the world is this young Miss in her harlequin cut slim jims of Terylene and wool. This fabric resists wrinkles and the slacks will keep their well-tailored look through years of hard wear. The striped Terylene tricot blouse is the same fabric as is used in men's shirtings. It can be washed and drip-dried with little or no ironing. The slacks are by Irving, the blouse by Lady Dundee. Terylene yarn by Canadian Industries Ltd.

Figure 100 The 'KUL-E-TUK' is an original Canadian design adapted from the traditional Parka of the Eastern Arctic Eskimos. Introduced recently for every member of the family, it is now manufactured under licence in the United States of America. Knitted fleeces of Orlon* acrylic fibre simulating caribou skins and brushed nylon are the most popular fabrics. Adaptation shown by Lydia Fashions Inc. of Montreal, was worn by the Canadian Women's Olympic Team at Squaw Valley, California. The peaked hood and back are cut in one piece. Yarn by DuPont of Canada.

**DuPont's registered trade mark for its acrylic fibre.*

Figure 101   Official Parade outfit for the opening-day ceremonies at the 1960 Winter Olympics consisted of a Hudson's Bay Blanket coat, red stretch nylon ski-slacks, Royal Canadian Mounted Police type hat of seal-skin and matching boots. The men's outfit was similar. The Canadian team's wardrobe was a highlight of a series of fashion shows at Montreal's first Winter Sports Fair. The yarns by DuPont of Canada.

Figure 102   Ski-jackets, 100 per cent silk knit nylon woven by Bruck Mills Ltd. Interlined with 'Bondicell' a lightweight indestructable material, lined with 100 per cent Bruck woven nylon. The nylon yarn by DuPont of Canada Ltd., the quilting by the Montreal Quilting Co. From Pedigree Manufacturing Co. Ltd., Montreal.

Figure 103   Ladies and men's Ski-jacket, 100 per cent cotton by Silk Knit Ltd., reversible to nylon. Interlined with Urethene foam. Hood concealed in collar and into back of the jacket. Two way zippers. In a range of patterns and colours. From Pedigree Manufacturing Co. Ltd., Montreal.

Figures 104 and 105   (*Left*) Two cotton (Guage 80) Guipure edgings. (*Right*) Gold Lurex embroidered on black nylon net. Flowers stitched on gold lamé and appliqued on. Designed and manufactured by Montreal Swiss Embroidery Works Ltd.

Figures 106 and 107   (*Top*) Cotton on organza (*Bottom*) Two colour design on organza. Stripe in green Lurex thread. Floral work in pink cotton. From Montreal Swiss Embroidery Works Ltd.

Figures 108, 109 and 110   (*Top*) Guipure decorative runner in heavy cotton yarn. (*Centre*) Four Guipure edgings in Guage 80 cotton. (*Bottom*) Schiffli type embroidery. The design worked in silk on cotton. Designed and manufactured by Montreal Swiss Embroidery Works Ltd.

Figures 111 and 112   (*Top*) Lingerie medallions on nylon sheer, using cotton embroidery. (*Bottom*) Large all-over floral design of heavy cotton yarn stitching on black satin. Designed and made by the Montreal Swiss Embroidery Works Ltd.

Figures 113 and 114   (*Left*) An all-over design using black Lurex thread on black organza. (*Right*) A two-colour design worked in cotton yarn on double-knit jersey wool. Designed and manufactured by the Montreal Swiss Embroidery Works Ltd.

ILLUSTRATIONS

FIG. I/2. *(top)* BY JEANNE D'ARC FORTIN *(bottom)* BY GEORGE EDWARD TREMBLEY

FIG. 3/4. *(top)* BY GRENFELL LABRADOR INDUSTRIES *(bottom)* BY MRS ULDERIC COLLARD

FIG. 5. BOARD ROOM OF CENTRALE D'ARTISANAT DU QUEBEC, MONTREAL

FIG. 6. GROUP OF HANDWOVEN "CATALOGNE" RUGS

FIG. 7. FROM SEARS-GOLICK (CANADA) FABRICS

FIG. 8/9. *(top)* FROM DALY & MORIN LTD, LACHINE, P.Q.
(bottom) FROM SHEFTEX CORPORATION, MONTREAL

FIG. IO. FROM RIVERDALE TOWN HOUSE FABRICS, MONTREAL

FIG. 11/12. FROM DALY & MORIN LTD, LACHINE, P.Q.

FIG. 13. FROM RIVERDALE TOWN HOUSE FABRICS, MONTREAL

FIG. 14/15. FROM DALY & MORIN LTD, LACHINE, P.Q.

FIG. 16. FROM A.B. CAYA LTD., KITCHENER, ONTARIO

FIG. 17/18. *(top)* FROM VAL-ABEL TEXTILES LTD, MONTREAL
(bottom) FROM DALY & MORIN LTD, LACHINE, P.Q.

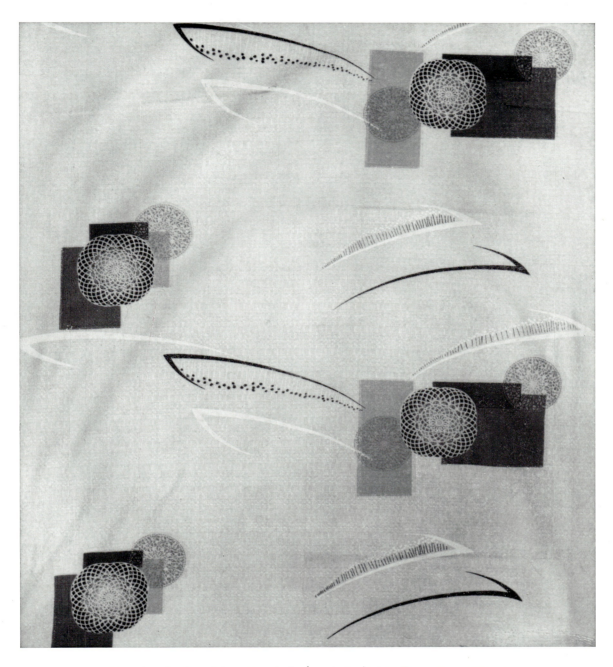

FIG. 19. FROM SEARS-GOLICK (CANADA) FABRICS, MONTREAL

FIG. 20. FROM DALY & MORIN LTD, LACHINE, P.Q.

FIG. 21/22. *(top)* FROM DALY & MORIN LTD, LACHINE, P.Q.
(bottom) FROM SHEFTEX CORPORATION, MONTREAL

FIG. 23/24. *(top)* FROM SHEFTEX CORPORATION, MONTREAL
(bottom) FROM SEARS-GOLICK (CANADA) FABRICS, MONTREAL

FIG. 25/26. FROM DALY & MORIN LTD, LACHINE, P.Q.

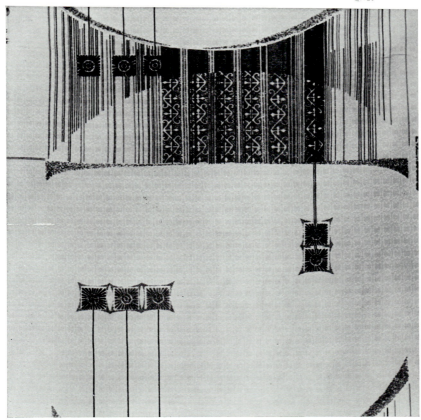

FIG. 27/28. FROM A.B. CAYA LTD, KITCHENER, ONTARIO

FIG. 29/30. *(top)* FROM RIVERDALE TOWN HOUSE FABRICS, MONTREAL
(bottom) FROM SEARS-GOLICK (CANADA) FABRICS, MONTREAL

FIG. 31/32. FROM DALY & MORIN LTD, LACHINE, P.Q.

FIG. 33/34. *(top)* FROM DALY & MORIN LTD, LACHINE, P.Q.
(bottom) FROM ST. LOUIS TEXTILES LTD, MONTREAL

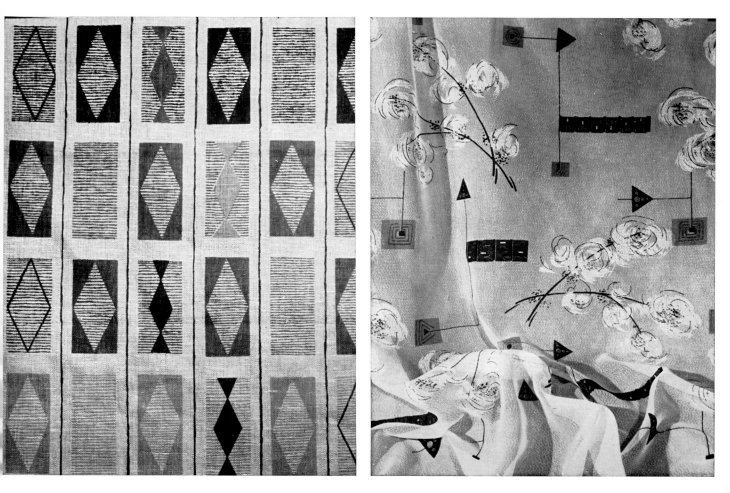

G. 35/36. *(left)* FROM A.B. CAYA LTD, KITCHENER, ONTARIO *(right)* FROM ST. LOUIS TEXTILES LTD, MONTREAL

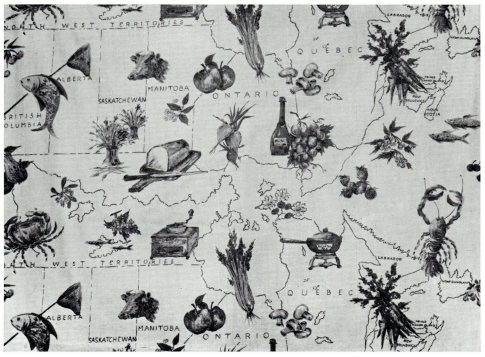

FIG. 37/38. FROM DALY & MORIN LTD, LACHINE, P.Q.

FIG. 39/42. *(top left and right)* FROM THE WABASSO COTTON CO LTD, MONTREAL
(bottom left and right) FROM A.B. CAYA LTD, KITCHENER, ONTARIO

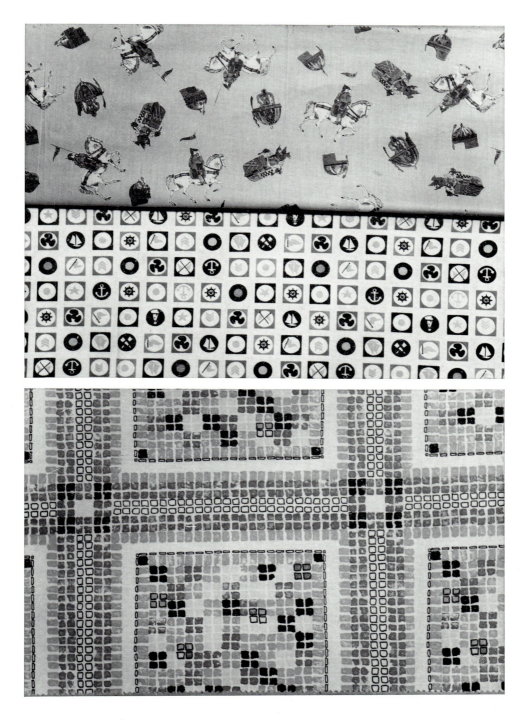

FIG. 43/45. FROM DOMINION TEXTILE CO, LTD, MONTREAL

FIG. 46/49. *(top)* ALL FROM CONSOLIDATED TEXTILES LTD, MONTREAL
(bottom) FROM DALY & MORIN LTD, LACHINE, P.Q.

FIG. 50/53. FROM CONSOLIDATED TEXTILES LTD, MONTREAL

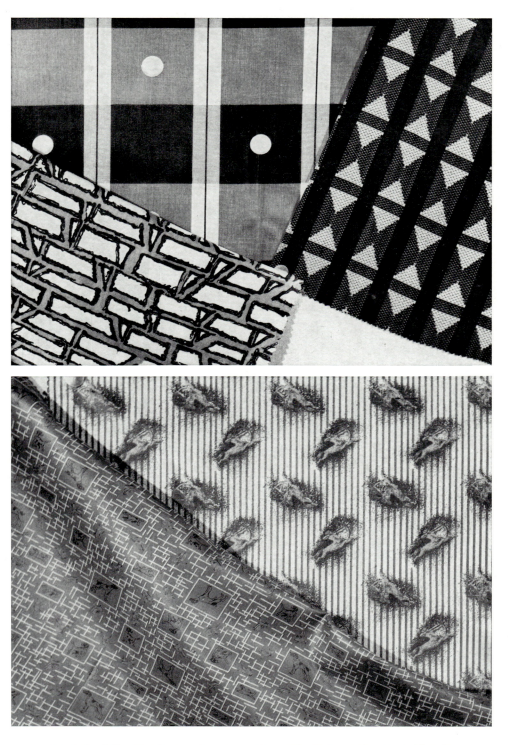

FIG. 54/58. FROM CONSOLIDATED TEXTILES LTD, MONTREAL

FIG. 59. FROM DOMINION TEXTILE CO, LTD, MONTREAL

FIG. 60/61. *(top)* FROM THE WABASSO COTTON CO, LTD, MONTREAL
(bottom) FROM SPRINGDALE MILLS LTD, MONTREAL

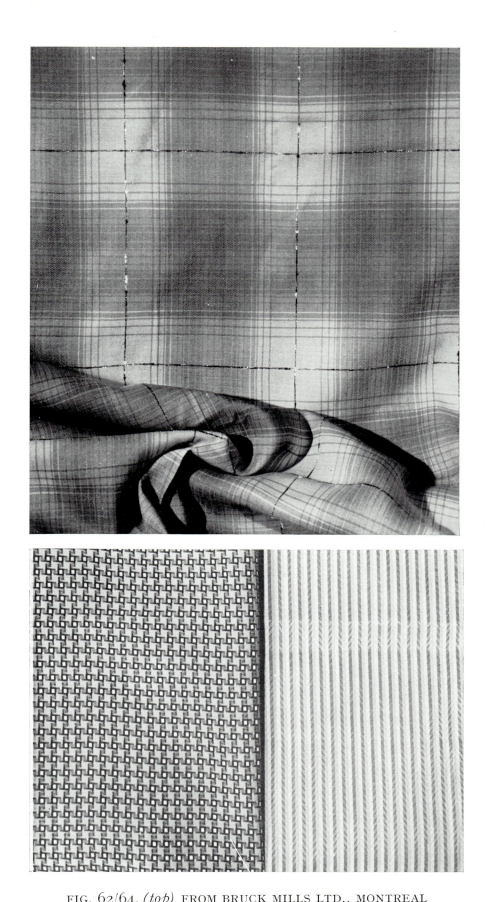

FIG. 62/64. *(top)* FROM BRUCK MILLS LTD., MONTREAL
(bottom) FROM CONSOLIDATED TEXTILES LTD, MONTREAL

FIG. 65/68. *(top)* BOTH FROM SHEFTEX CORPORATION, MONTREAL
(bottom left and right) FROM ARTEX WOOLLENS LTD, HESPELER, ONTARIO

FIG. 69/72. FROM KAREN BULOW LTD, MONTREAL, P.Q.

FIG. 73/76. FROM ARTEX WOOLLENS LTD, HESPELER, ONTARIO

FIG. 77/80. *(top)* BOTH FROM TEXTILE WEAVERS LTD, GRAND'MERE, P.Q.
(bottom) THE TOP FABRIC FROM J. A. HUMPHREY & SON LTD, MONCTON, N.B.
AND BOTTOM FROM ARTEX WOOLLENS LTD, HESPELER, ONTARIO

FIG. 81/86. *(top)* FROM J. A. HUMPHREY & SON, LTD, TEXTILE WEAVERS LTD & ARTEX WOOLLENS LTD *(see descriptive notes)*

FIG. 87/88. *(bottom)* FROM ARTEX WOOLLENS LTD, HESPELER, ONTARIO

FIG. 89/90 *(top)* FROM ARTEX WOOLLENS LTD, HESPELER, ONTARIO
(bottom) FROM BURLINGTON INDUSTRIES (CANADA) LTD

FIG. 91/92. *(top)* FROM IDEAL SPREAD COMPANY, MONTREAL
(bottom) FROM BURLINGTON INDUSTRIES (CANADA) LTD

FIG. 93/95. FROM IDEAL SPREAD COMPANY, MONTREAL

FIG. 96/97. FROM ROBERT GENS & CO, LTD, MONTREAL

FIG. 98/99. *(left)* FROM HARVEY WOODS & DUPONT OF CANADA
(right) SLACKS BY IRVING, BLOUSE BY LADY DUNDEE & YARNS BY CANADIAN INDUSTRIES LTD

FIG. 100/101. FROM LYDIA FASHIONS INC., MONTREAL & DUPONT OF CANADA

FIG. 102/103. FROM PEDIGREE MANUFACTURING CO, LTD, MONTREAL

FIG. 104/105. FROM THE MONTREAL SWISS EMBROIDERY WORKS LTD

FIG. 106/107. FROM THE MONTREAL SWISS EMBROIDERY WORKS LTD

FIG. 108/110. FROM THE MONTREAL SWISS EMBROIDERY WORKS LTD

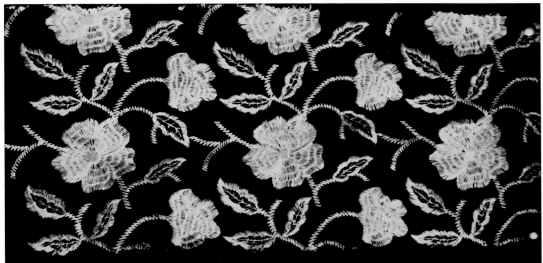

FIG. III/112. FROM THE MONTREAL SWISS EMBROIDERY WORKS LTD

FIG. 113/114. FROM THE MONTREAL SWISS EMBROIDERY WORKS LTD